Wonders Built by Humans

MACHU PICCHU

Sloane Gould

CREATED BY Humans

Published in 2026 by The Rosen Publishing Group, Inc.
2544 Clinton Street, Buffalo, NY 14224

First Edition

Editor: Caitie McAneney
Designer: Rachel Rising

Photo Credits: Cover, Sandro Sandoval /Shutterstock.com; Cover, (series background) Yuliya Chsherbakova/Shutterstock.com; p. 5 David Ionut/Shutterstock.com; p. 7 Tibbou/Shutterstock.com; p. 9 SL-Photography/Shutterstock.com; p. 11 Ivan_off/Shutterstock.com; p. 11 Rainer Lesniewski/Shutterstock.com; p. 13 Jerome Stubbs/Shutterstock.com; p. 15 Peter Hermes Furian/Shutterstock.com; p. 16 nuel_cruz/Shutterstock.com; p. 17 Terri Butler Photography/Shutterstock.com; p. 19 Everton Lourenco/Shutterstock.com; p. 21 BETO SANTILLAN/Shutterstock.com; p. 23 https://commons.wikimedia.org/wiki/File:HiramBingham.jpg; p. 25 Yury Zap/Shutterstock.com; p. 27 Santiago Marquez/Shutterstock.com; p. 29 AYO Production/Shutterstock.com.

Cataloging-in-Publication Data

Names: Gould, Sloane.
Title: Machu Picchu / Sloane Gould.
Description: Buffalo, NY : Created by Humans, an imprint of Rosen Publishing, 2026. | Series: Wonders built by humans | Includes glossary and index.
Identifiers: ISBN 9781534552999 (pbk.) | ISBN 9781534553002 (library bound) | ISBN 9781534553019 (ebook)
Subjects: LCSH: Inca architecture--Juvenile literature. | Machu Picchu Site (Peru)--Juvenile literature
Classification: LCC F3429.1.M3 G685 2026 | DDC 985.37--dc23

Manufactured in China

CPSIA Compliance Information: Batch #QWCBH26. For Further Information contact Rosen Publishing at 1-800-237-9932.

CONTENTS

ANCIENT RUINS

Humans have built amazing things on Earth, from the tallest skyscrapers to the longest bridges. Each year, engineering and tools become more advanced. That makes building wonders even easier.

However, humans have been building for a long time. Long before modern tools and **technology**, ancient **civilizations** built huge cities. They used whatever they had, from mud to wood to stone.

Many ancient buildings have been lost to time. However, some ruins stand today. They have a lot to teach us about what the world was like for the people who came before us. One shining example of ancient **ingenuity** can be found in the Incan ruins of Machu Picchu.

The Inca used their human genius to troubleshoot this tricky landscape and build Machu Picchu.

A WONDROUS CITY

Machu Picchu isn't just a single building. It's a whole city! It stands in the Andes Mountains in south-central Peru. It included homes, plazas, temples, farms, and more. It's important because it's one of the only ancient sites in South America to be found intact. It's also important because its **design** is a marvel of engineering.

Machu Picchu was about 50 miles (80.5 km) away from the Incan capital of Cuzco (or Cusco). Surrounded by forests and mountains, it remained hidden for hundreds of years. This kept it safe from Spanish **conquistadors**. While the Inca were wiped out, Machu Picchu stood as proof of their advanced civilization.

WOW!

Machu Picchu means "Old Peak" in Quechua, the language of the Inca.

Machu Picchu is high in the mountains—
nearly 8,000 feet (2,438.4 m) above sea level!

THE INCREDIBLE INCA

The Incan Empire stretched about 2,500 miles (4,023.4 km) along the western coast of South America. It covered areas from today's countries of Ecuador down to Chile. The Inca grew their empire by conquering other Native peoples for land. They hit their peak in the early 1500s.

The Incan capital city was Cuzco, which was built around 1100. The Inca also built amazing systems of roads, temples, and bridges. By the late 1400s, the empire had about 12 million people. Most of the Inca herded llamas and alpacas, or grew crops for their families. Royals were treated as gods, living in golden palaces.

WOW!

The Inca had the largest empire in the world in the 1500s.

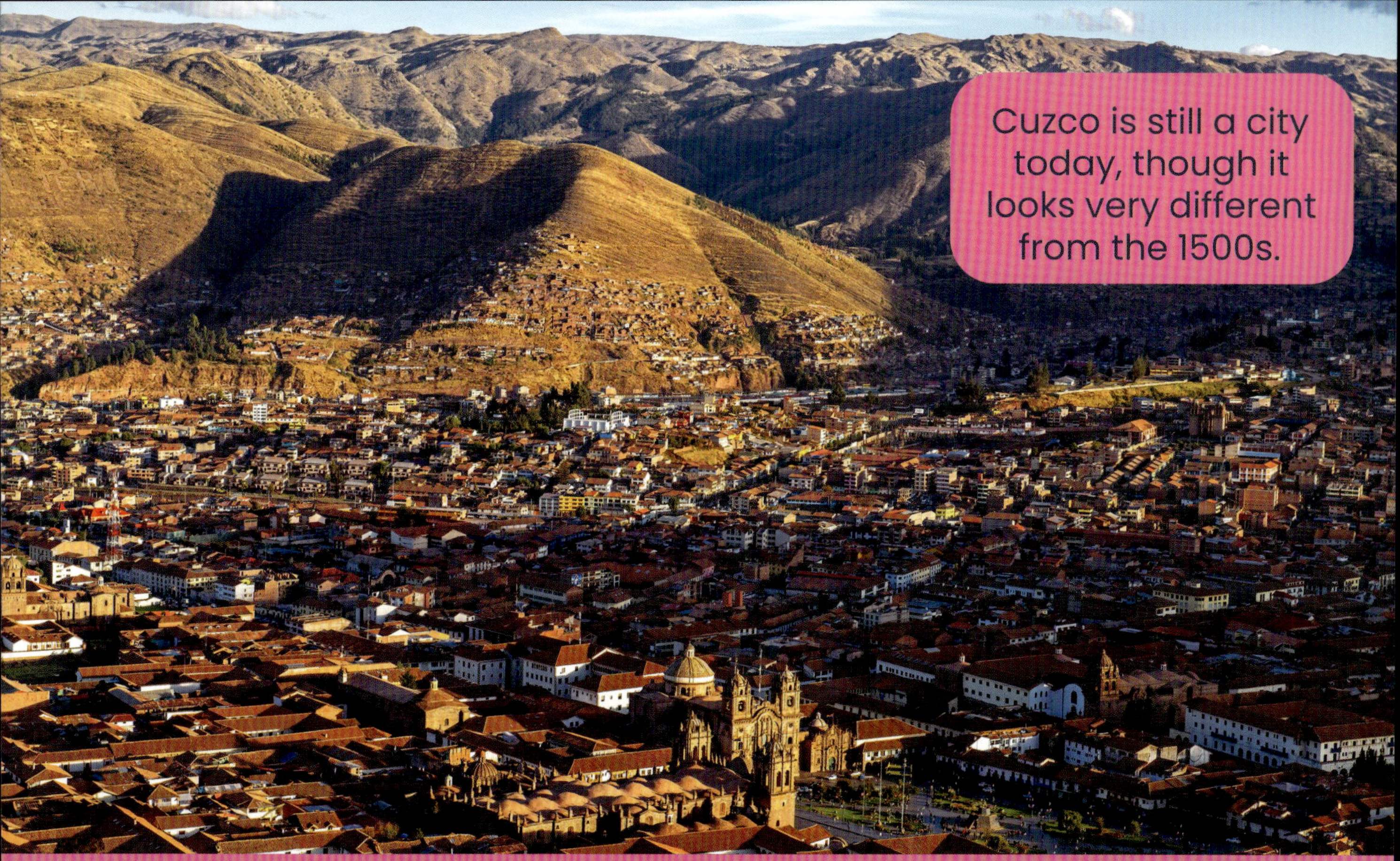

Cuzco is still a city today, though it looks very different from the 1500s.

The End of the Inca

Though the Incan Empire was large and powerful, it met its end in the 1500s. In 1526, a civil war started in the empire when the two sons of an Incan king fought for power. People who had been conquered by the Inca also started to fight back against them. To make matters worse, deadly smallpox spread quickly as Europeans arrived in South America. Soon after, gold-hungry Spanish arrived to find the golden temples of Cuzco. In 1533, conquistador Francisco Pizarro killed the Incan emperor. It was the end of the civilization.

THE LAYOUT

Machu Picchu was built between two tall mountain peaks. It was split into two parts. One part was urban—the city section. It included thousands of stone steps and many walkways that connected important places, such as houses, plazas, and temples. A landmark was Intihuatana, a stone pillar that probably acted as a kind of ancient calendar.

The other part of Machu Picchu was for farming. The farms were built into the slopes of the mountain using a technique called terrace farming. Terraces are fields that look like steps cut into the mountain slopes. Farmers grew sweet potatoes, corn, and more.

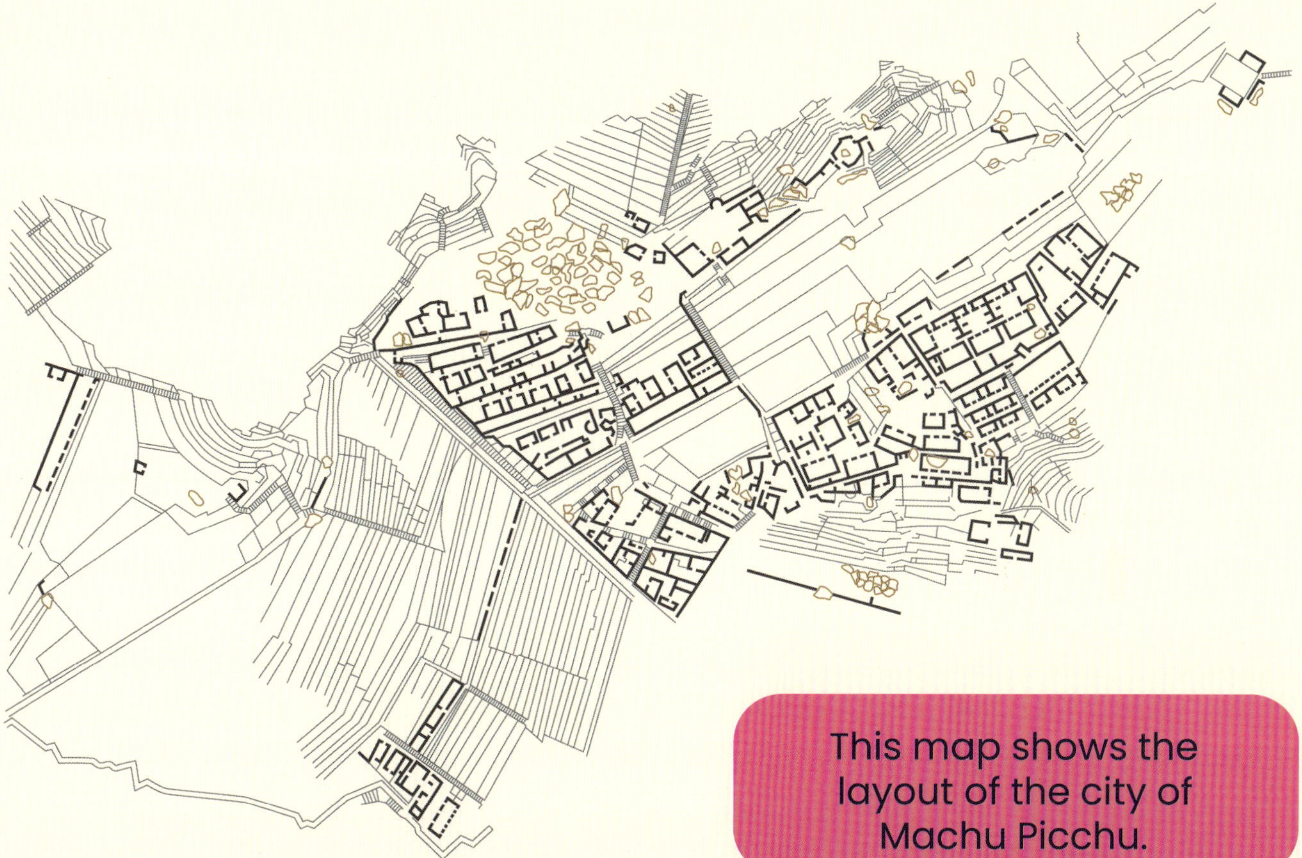

This map shows the layout of the city of Machu Picchu.

BUILDING A WONDER

Why was Machu Picchu built? Many people believe it was built for a powerful Incan emperor named Pachacuti. It could have been a smaller mountain city to escape the busy, noisy capital of Cuzco.

Machu Picchu was built around the year 145. It could house between 500 and 750 people. While we don't know who designed and built Machu Picchu, we do know that they had advanced ideas and skills. The design shows advanced knowledge of farming, landscaping, stonework, and **astronomy**. They fit the stones together without mortar to bind them. Because of the **precision** of the fit between stones, the buildings held strong.

The way stones fit together is one reason Machu Picchu has stood the test of time.

WOW!

The Inca built Machu Picchu without the use of iron or steel tools!

EARTHQUAKES? NO PROBLEM!

Peru has a lot of earthquakes. That's because it's located on two fault lines. The ancient Inca knew this all too well, and probably took it into account as they built. In fact, some scientists have found that some of the structures at Machu Picchu were subject to two earthquakes as they were being constructed. The builders seemed to adjust their building **techniques** accordingly.

The reason Machu Picchu has stood strong through earthquakes is because of the way the stones fit together. The blocks lock together tightly. When an earthquake happens, the blocks bounce a bit, then settle back into place.

This is a map of the Pacific Ring of Fire.

The Pacific Ring of Fire

Peru is located on the Pacific Ring of Fire. That's a 25,000-mile (40,000 km) horseshoe-shaped area around the Pacific Ocean where there are many volcanoes and earthquakes due to shifting **tectonic plates**. Around 90 percent of all the earthquakes on Earth happen in the Ring of Fire! The Andes Mountains, where Machu Picchu stands, are the result of plate tectonics. The ancient Inca likely had hundreds of years of knowledge and skills for building earthquake-**resistant** structures.

TEMPLE OF THE SUN

The Temple of the Sun is one of the greatest structures in Machu Picchu. It was one of the most sacred, or holy, temples in the city. It was used only by the **elites** and priests. They worshipped their Sun God, Inti. They may have done **sacrifices** there. It was also likely a royal tomb.

The Temple of the Sun was built out of granite rock. It had a circular shape with a trapezoid-shaped window. Once each year, at the winter solstice, sunlight would shine through that window. It would light up a large stone for the Inca festival of Inti Raymi each June.

INTI

The Temple of the Sun shows us just how much the Inca knew about astronomy and the cycle of the sun.

PILLAR WITH A PURPOSE

Another landmark in Machu Picchu is Intihuatana. It's also known as the "Hitching Post of the Sun." This pillar is close to the main plaza, or gathering space, in Machu Picchu.

Like the Temple of the Sun, this structure shows that the Inca knew a lot about nature's cycles. It acted as a sort of large stone sundial. It had a 6-foot (1.8 m) tall pedestal and pillar. It probably helped the Inca keep track of the seasons. It may have helped them figure out when to plant and harvest their crops. It may have also been used for ceremonies to honor the Sun God, Inti.

This is Intihuatana in Machu Picchu.

SURVIVING CENTURIES

How has Machu Picchu stood the test of time? It has survived earthquakes and bad weather. It outlived the Incan Empire by centuries.

The secret to Machu Picchu's survival is its strong materials and smart design. It is proof of the creative genius of the Inca. By working with the mountainous landscape, they set the structures up for success. Perhaps one of the greatest secrets to Machu Picchu's survival is the fact that it *was* a secret. The Spanish didn't know about it—so they never conquered it. In fact, no one but locals knew about Machu Picchu for hundreds of years.

It's not easy to get to Machu Picchu! This helped keep it hidden from people who may have destroyed it.

UNCOVERING MACHU PICCHU

The story of Machu Picchu's construction shows just how smart and creative the Inca were. Discovering Machu Picchu is its own story! The city had been hidden by the mountains and jungle that surrounded it. Plants had grown over the spot as well. The only people who knew about it were the locals.

Then, in 1911, a Yale University teacher and explorer named Hiram Bingham set out to find it. He'd heard rumors about a lost Incan city in Peru. He made his way through the jungle until he found farmers who would lead him to Machu Picchu.

WOW!

At first, Hiram Bingham thought he'd found a different lost city called Vilcabamba.

Bingham traveled through the Andes Mountains for many years, learning about ancient cultures.

Hiram Bingham

Hiram Bingham was born in 1875 in Honolulu, Hawaii. He had traveled through mountains for much his life. In July 1911, he led an expedition from Yale University to find "the lost city of the Incas." Once he found Machu Picchu, he led another expedition to **excavate** it. He wrote many books about his expeditions, including *Inca Land* and *Lost City of the Incas*. He later served as a senator and the governor of Connecticut.

VISITING MACHU PICCHU

How can you get to Machu Picchu? It's quite the journey! First you fly to Cuzco, Peru. Then, you get on a train. It'll take you to a town at the base of Machu Picchu called Aguas Calientes. You can take a tour of Machu Picchu with a tour guide from here.

Other people want to travel more like the Inca. They hike from Cuzco to Machu Picchu! They take trails such as the Salkantay Trek or Inca Trail. The hike usually takes between five to eight days. It's not an easy hike! You have to be willing to deal with hard exercise and high altitude.

WOW!

Altitude is the height above sea level. High altitudes can make some people feel sick or struggle to breathe.

People who take the Inca Trail can see many Inca ruins as they hike.

A WORLD WONDER

People didn't know that Machu Picchu wasn't Vilcabamba, the "lost city," until the mid-1900s! It was another lost city, one with its own special design and history. Archaeologists have spent lots of time studying the ruins and learning more about the people who left them.

In 1983, Machu Picchu became a World Heritage Site. **UNESCO** writes that it "was probably the most amazing urban creation of the Inca Empire at its height." It is a monument to human creativity and genius. People come from all over the world to experience Machu Picchu in person!

About 1.5 million people visit Machu Picchu each year!

YOU CAN DESIGN IT!

Imagine you are tasked with creating a self-sustaining city in the mountains. It needs to be strong enough to withstand earthquakes. It needs to have room for farming and buildings for many people to gather. Time to think like an engineer!

Ask yourself:

- What materials will I use?
- What buildings are important to my community?
- What will buildings be used for?
- How can I make it stand for centuries?

Sketch out some plans for your building on a separate sheet of paper.

Bonus: Share your ideas with friends, or write a short story set in your city!

You can be a creative genius too!

GLOSSARY

astronomy: The study of objects and matter in outer space.

civilization: Organized society with written records and laws.

conquistador: A Spanish conqueror or adventurer.

design: A plan for something.

elite: Someone from a high social class.

excavate: To dig and remove earth in order to find something.

ingenuity: Skill or cleverness that allows people to solve problems and create inventions.

precision: The quality or state of being exact.

resistant: Able to stay unaffected when faced with something challenging.

sacrifice: The act of killing as an offering to please a god.

technique: A certain way of doing something; a particular skill or ability that someone uses to perform a job.

technology: Using science, engineering, and other industries to invent useful tools or to solve problems. Also a machine, piece of equipment, or method created by technology.

tectonic plate: One of the moveable masses of rock that make up Earth's surface.

UNESCO: Stands for United Nations Educational, Scientific, and Cultural Organization.

FOR MORE INFORMATION

BOOKS

Bradshaw, Eleanor. *20 Things You Didn't Know About Machu Picchu.* Buffalo, NY: PowerKids Press, 2025.

Havemeyer, Janie. *A Day in the Inca Empire.* Minneapolis, MN: Grasshopper, 2025.

Sonneborn, Scott. *Machu Picchu, Lost City of the Incas.* North Mankato, MN: Capstone Press, 2025.

WEBSITES

Inca Civilization
kids.nationalgeographic.com/history/article/inca-civilization
Explore amazing facts about the ancient Inca.

Machu Picchu
kids.britannica.com/kids/article/Machu-Picchu/346167
Learn more about Machu Picchu with Britannica Kids.

Machu Picchu 101
www.youtube.com/watch?v=cnMa-Sm9H4k
Visit Machu Picchu in this exciting video by National Geographic!

Publisher's note to educators and parents: Our editors have carefully reviewed these websites to ensure that they are suitable for students. Many websites change frequently, however, and we cannot guarantee that a site's future contents will continue to meet our high standards of quality and educational value. Be advised that students should be closely supervised whenever they access the internet.

INDEX